ITALY

Metro Books
122 Fifth Avenue
New York, NY 10011

ISBN: 978-0-7607-8114-2

Printed and bound in China

10 9 8 7 6 5 4

Venice, The Redentore.
Pisa, the Duomo and the Tower.
Rome, a panoramic view.

TEXT Ettore Pettinaroli

ITALY

METRO BOOKS
NEW YORK

Who knows whether the first modern rhapsodists of Italy's wonders, such as Goethe or Byron, would recognize the cities or landscapes they fell in love with, and made so attractive to their readers? What would Princess Sissy have to say about her Dolomites? Would the British mountaineers, among the first to scale the Alps, repeat those legendary climbs?

ITALY *land of the senses*

We believe they would. Centuries have passed, but on the threshold of the third

millennium, Italy is still the Bel Paese. The peninsula continues to offer the world

the architectural and natural wonders that have been its fortune.

Each day, Italy sends millions of postcards straight to the hearts of travelers,

romantics, scholars, gourmets, and art lovers. Those postcards carry pictures

of St Mark's Square and the Grand Canal in Venice, the Colosseum and the Imperial

Forum in Rome, and of Etna's smoking crater in Sicily.

They show Tuscany and the splendid historic center of Florence, the Leaning

Tower of Pisa, and the hills of Chianti and Val d'Orcia. Nor should we forget

the sea that surrounds the peninsula on three sides. Studded with history

and heritage–rich islands like Sicily, or the celebrity promised land of Sardinia,

the sea also offers tiny Capri, the obligatory destination of travelers in search

of romance, and the Tremiti archipelago in the Adriatic, a haven for intellectuals

and uncomplicated nature lovers.

Then there are the mountains, especially Mont Blanc, Europe's highest peak,

and the distinctive pyramid of the Matterhorn. Over in the north east,

the rock faces of the Dolomites change color with the day's passing hours,

according to the angle of the sun's ever–shifting caress.

But these postcards are no longer enough. They fail to tell the story of Italy's new old treasures, the traditions that have been tenaciously observed and astutely re-interpreted. The ability to conserve a cultural heritage, while keeping it relevant to the present day, is a very Italian skill. It can be seen at work in the kitchen, or during historic re–enactments, but it is also evident in the world of work.

Travelers to Venice or the Venetian lagoon will not be able to restrict themselves to Saint Mark's Square and thereabouts. Now, they will feel an urge to investigate the workshops of the master glassblowers of Murano, and the lacemakers of Burano, and explore the gondolas under construction in the squeri, or boatyards.

They won't have any trouble. No one has any secrets, and everything is shown off proudly by enthusiastic craft workers. The same is true on the high-mountain pastures of Valle d'Aosta, where dairy workers make subtly delicious cheeses, or the flatlands of Campania, home of the buffalo mozzarella that has no equal elsewhere. Each village, from the north of Italy to the south, has its own treasure. It lives from that treasure, and tells its story through it, fueling the legend of an extraordinary country. Italy is a land to be experienced, not just admired.

VENICE

You couldn't invent a city like Venice today. You might be able to clone its monuments, ape its dialect, and copy the festivals and rituals. But there would still be something missing, rather like the secret ingredient that makes a top chef's special recipe truly memorable. That something could be so well concealed that it may not even exist, or it could be flaunted so outrageously as to become invisible. There's no point in straining to find the answer. It's much better simply to enjoy the marvels of a unique city without asking too many questions. Venice is so magical that it transforms what elsewhere would be annoying floods into a tourist attraction (preceding pages: high water in Saint Mark's Square). It is a city that enjoys being courted, and even caressed by anyone who shows a minimum of affection. Yet Venice never quite goes all the way. She knows when enough is enough.

Saint Mark's Basilica
As soon as they arrive in the lagoon, tourists head straight for Saint Mark's Square, which means it gets more crowded in the morning. In contrast, thoughtful visitors know that the afternoon sun bathes the Basilica (above: a view of the interior) in the light that photographers most appreciate. So be patient, and devote the early hours of the day to other sights. Later on, Saint Mark's Square will be waiting for you in all its dazzling finery. Don't be in a hurry. Take your time discovering it bit by bit. Be impressed by the imposing entrance surmounted by the legendary bronze horses. Admire the delicacy of the sumptuous mosaic decorations (left). Close your guidebook, and let your heart show you the way. Reflect that all this majesty has no author for no one knows who designed it. Many scholars say that the builder resembles the seated figure in the central archway, crutches to hand, who looks as if he is biting his hands. The Basilica was severely criticized from the start because of stability problems that were immediately apparent. Still, it doesn't look too bad for a 900-year-old.

VENICE

San Giorgio

San Giorgio Maggiore (above: viewed from a window in the Doge's Palace) is an island only in name. Venetians have always considered it a sort of architectural extension of nearby Saint Mark's Square. From the forecourt of Palladio's church dedicated to Saint George, the eye takes in one after the other the great architect's Zitelle and Redentore churches, the Baroque Salute church, the Grand Canal, and Riva degli Schiavoni, which leads into Saint Mark's Square. It's not just a postcard scene. The prestige and spiritual stature of San Giorgio are borne out by the conclave that was held here from December 1799 to March 1800. The cardinals had fled from Rome, where Napoleon Bonaparte was on the loose, and landed at San Giorgio under the protective wing of Franz II of Austria. Pius VII, elected to the papacy in this highly atmospheric setting, managed to deal with Napoleon without submitting to the Austrians. Was this a divine miracle or a Venetian one?

Doge's Palace

As the civil and political hub of Saint Mark's Square, the role of the Doge's Palace was not restricted to housing the governors of the Most Serene Republic with the appropriate pomp. The palace had to impress, or rather dazzle, foreign dignitaries visiting Venice. That is the reason for the magnificent staircases and halls, and the grandeur of the art. A formidable example is provided by the Paradise completed by Jacopo and Domenico Tintoretto. It is the largest canvas in the world, covering an entire wall of the Sala del Maggior Consiglio (right: the ceiling). Following pages: The windows of the historic Caffè Florian, also situated in Saint Mark's Square.

VENICE
Ca' d'Oro

No one knows what happened
to the gold cladding of the
15th-century façade of this palazzo,
which looks onto the Grand Canal.
But then, what does it matter?
The name, Ca' d'Oro (Golden
House), remains to remind us of
when its exterior was pretentious,
to say the least. The charm
of this palazzo, one of the most
significant examples of Venetian
High Gothic, is not lost even
on the crew of the traditional punt
plying the canal. Despite their
physical effort, the rowers seem
to be turning to admire it one
more time. Ca' d'Oro is a reminder
of the days when Venice's noble
families vied with each other
to build the most elegant and
impressive home. Today, we can
enjoy the fruits of those contests
as passive yet excited observers.
There is no answer to the
question, "Which is the loveliest?"
They all are.

VENICE

Sant'Anna

The Venice of the Venetians still survives, and rightly so. Lively and proud, it takes no notice of the invading tourists, who generally restrict themselves to well-defined routes. But should you happen to take a wrong turn to discover the Venetians. It is no great effort. You might, for example, be at Sant'Anna (left), in the Castello and Arsenale area. The clothes hanging out to dry speak volumes for the complete unconcern felt by their owners for the postcard Venice of out-of-towners. Yet even here there is no lack of monuments. Take the 14th-century church, with monastery, of Sant'Anna, deconsecrated in the 19th century, and converted into a hospital for the navy. It is said that it was here that two daughters of Jacopo Tintoretto took their vows before embroidering a silk cloth with one of the Crucifixions their father painted. In completing this enormous task, one of the two young nuns ruined her eyesight.

Burano

Once, Burano was the island of merchants. Then, it became the island of lace, thanks to the skill of the local women. They were also noted for having invented the punto in aria needlelace technique, and their bravura is well illustrated by the lacework articles on sale in the island's shops. Over the centuries, Burano has preserved its popular atmosphere. It has freshened up the colored façades of the houses (above), and reinvented a role for itself. Burano has become an oasis of serenity, and a refuge even on those days when Venice is at its most crowded and chaotic.

Squero

Oar power. That was once the only way to get around Venice, a city where the streets are paved with water. Founded on a thousand islands, Venice even today has nowhere to park a car. There are only poles and quays in the canal outside the houses, and everybody moves around by boat.

Since Venice produces only the extraordinary, its inhabitants travel in extraordinary vessels - gondolas - constructed with all the technical tweaks that sailing round such a unique environment requires. The squeri (above), the boatyards where highly skillful craft workers create these jewels, have never closed, and the demand for new gondolas is still high. To understand how Venice finds energy to overcome every adversity, visit a squero. Every moment in the working day of these artists is a declaration of evident, eternal love for their city.

Gondolas

They flit lightly over the canals, silent and agile. Brightly colored ones, decorated with gold and velvet, greet the tourists who clamber on board in Saint Mark's Square (above), while plainer, haughtier ones are used by the native Venetians. Gondolas seem to lean over to one side, as if about to capsize. But that asymmetry is the secret of their stability. They are designed to be steered by a single oarsman, so they have to be built like that to counterbalance his weight. This is especially necessary when the oarsman pulls all the stops out for a race, or one of the historic regattas (right) held on the Grand Canal.

Murano

Every day, the master glassblowers
of Murano play with fire. It was
to avoid the risk of fire from their
constantly burning furnaces
that in 1291, Venice's glassworks
were moved to the island of
Murano. The move made the
island's fortune. Since then,
Murano has been synonymous
with artistic glassware all over
the world. In many of the
glassworks, visitors can see at
first hand how glass is worked,
and how vases, murrines,
lamps, sculptures, simple plates,
and elaborately complex creations
are made. Every transformation
of an incandescent blob emerging
from the furnace looks like
a miracle. But the most surprising,
and consoling, thing is the number
of young people at work.
It's almost a fashion, and a very
welcome one.

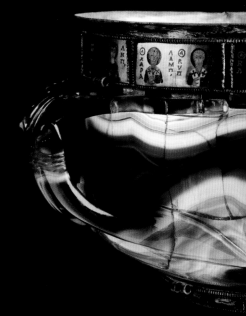

Treasure of Saint Mark

The Emperor's Cup (above right)
is one of the most valuable items
in the Treasure of Saint Mark that
can be viewed inside the Basilica.
Right: A Venetian Carnival mask.
For two weeks each year,
the city's calli and campielli are
invaded by costumed visitors,
most of them inspired by the
moments of glory in Venice's
history. Together, they put on
an extemporary, but extremely
entertaining, open-air
re-enactment of the city's
past grandeur.
Following pages: The bell tower
of the cathedral of Torcello,
one of the loveliest islands
in the Venetian lagoon, seems
to want to ferry the citizens
of Venice to the Alps.

CORTINA

Is it still possible to dream
at Cortina d'Ampezzo? Of course
it is, as a glance at the
photographs on this page will
confirm. The Queen of the
Dolomites may have been assailed
by a clientele that prefers
celebrity razzle-dazzle to the
silence of the mountains,
but Cortina continues to enchant
those who approach her in the
right spirit. She wins hearts
forever by day, thanks
to incomparable panoramas
(above: Becco di Mezzodì),
and by night with a vast selection
of flavors and aromas rich
in authentic local tradition.
For those who prefer the night
life, there is plenty on offer,
although it is impossible to get
into the legendary private parties.
Still, Cortina has other solutions.
And you have all the following
day to get back into shape.

LAKE GARDA

Much in favor with foreign
visitors, Lake Garda has recently
been rediscovered by Italians.
The towns on the eastern shore
have produced trump cards that
no one knew they had until
recently. The ace up the lakeside's
sleeve is gastronomy. Locals have
promoted their vineyards and olive
groves, as well as outdoor
activities. Mountain biking
is a new favorite as a dry-land
alternative to sailing or windsurfing.
Of course, between a plate
of something tasty and a bike trip,
you can enjoy fantastic scenery,
for example Punta San Virgilio
in the municipality of Garda.
You only have to look at
the photographs on the following
pages to experience the emotions
of guests like Maria Ludovika
of Austria in the early 19th
century, Winston Churchill,
Laurence Olivier, and HRH Prince
Charles of Great Britain.

VICENZA
La Rotonda

Try calling it by its real name, Villa Almerico. It won't respond, that's for sure. By now, the house itself is convinced its name is La Rotonda, the one it is known by all round the world. The most celebrated of the homes designed by Andrea Palladio is in Vicenza. It owes its notoriety to the round dome that was constructed after the great man died in 1580. Here, Palladio's genius finds its finest expression in the quest for perfect symmetry. As a result, La Rotonda has become a sort of icon to the ideals of the Renaissance. Its prestigious formality encourages meditation, but it is not really a place you to live in, or from which to manage your affairs.

Yet, that is probably what Cardinal Almerico wanted when he commissioned the project. La Rotonda is what he got. How much did it cost? Apart from the considerable sum of money he spent, it cost him his now-forgotten name.

RIVIERA DEL BRENTA
Strà

It's called the Riviera del Brenta, even though it is just the bank of a small river that flows rather unimaginatively through the fields separating Padua from the Adriatic Sea. Its nearness to the Most Serene Republic meant that this riverbank was the preferred out-of-town refuge of the Venetian aristocracy. Patricians built their country residences here in an almost unbroken succession.

There are dozens of these grand, and clearly Palladian, villas embellishing the countryside with their sumptuous façades (right: Villa Foscarini, now Villa Negrelli, at Strà). Can I make a suggestion? Take a trip on one of the boats that ply the Brenta's placid waters, and view them from the river.

VERONA

The tragic story of Romeo and Juliet has turned Verona into the "city of lovers." That reputation has of course encouraged tourism, but it is a narrow view in the eyes of the local population, whose history is far more ancient and significant. Take, for example, the spectacular Roman Arena (right: a view). Situated in the very center of Verona, the Arena enjoys excellent health, despite its years and the prestigious theatrical and musical events it regularly hosts. From here, it is only a few minutes' walk to Juliet's house in Via Cappello. It matters little that Shakespeare's heroine was only a fictional character, and that the much-photographed balcony was added to the building only in 1935. Legends will have the better of truth, particularly if they are credible ones. So why not pretend that the legend is true, for once?

FANES DOLOMITES

Every evening, the walls of the Dolomites at Fanes burst into flame (following pages). It is a fire that does no damage, and in fact is eagerly awaited. Fingers are crossed in case a cloud should slip in between the sunset and the rock. Spectacular sights like this have forged the legend of the Dolomites, the chain of mountains that straddles Veneto and Trentino Alto Adige. Tourist resorts have sprung up at the foot of these flaming cliffs. Popular all year round with skiers and climbers, they are also a magnet for discriminating gourmets in search of authentic flavors, and for lovers of beauty. Whatever the visitors have come to do, at a certain point in the afternoon, they will raise their eyes to see the fire.

MILAN

The porticos that skirt round
Piazza del Duomo (preceding
pages) seem to be purpose built
so that the Milanese can get to
their next appointment quickly
and comfortably. People in Milan
are in a hurry, as everyone knows.
They haven't always been, though.
Completing their marvelous Gothic
Duomo, surmounted by its statue
of the city's symbolic Madonnina,
took the Milanese five whole
centuries. Romanesque,
Renaissance, Art Nouveau,
and Futurist architecture are all
represented in Milan by excellent,
if not always well-known,
examples (above: detail of the
15th-century façade of the State
University, formerly the Ospedale
Maggiore). Milan also looks
to the future. The Teatro alla Scala
has just been restructured.
New developments are going
ahead to create new, futuristic
urban areas. Will the Milanese
be able to wait for them?

Castello Sforzesco
This green, silent city is not the
Milan you were expecting.
If it wasn't for the soaring Torre
del Filarete, which dominates
the Castello Sforzesco complex
and makes the location instantly
identifiable, you might think
that you were standing in front
of some elegant, isolated country
house. Yet the frantic hubbub
of Piazza del Duomo is only ten
minutes away. Following pages:
The vault of Galleria Vittorio
Emanuele II. Milan's elegant social
hub links Piazza del Duomo
to Piazza della Scala. The iron
and glass dome over the central
octagon is 47 meters high
and 37 across.

trampling by thousands of pairs of shoes (left). This covered downtown crossroads is on everyone's route, wherever they are going. Those with time on their hands - and a platinum card in their wallet - head for the fashion district and the dazzling, ultra-exclusive shop windows only a few hundred meters from Piazza Scala. Via Manzoni, Via della Spiga, Via Montenapoleone, and Via Sant'Andrea are the sides of Italy's and, they say in Milan, the world's most elegant quadrilateral. Don't look for designers here. Creatives prefer more tranquil surroundings, and rarely venture into the quadrilateral. But you can admire their work for nothing in the long succession of boutiques. This is the Milan that leaves you gasping for breath.

The Navigli

It leaves the river Ticino just below Lake Maggiore and crosses the loveliest part of the Lombard countryside before entering the heart of Milan. Passing under a bridge, it flows into the Darsena, next to Porta Ticinese. Then it says goodbye to the metropolis and heads south to Pavia, where it rejoins the Ticino. Until it reaches the Darsena, it is called the Naviglio Grande, becoming the Naviglio Pavese thereafter. The Navigli, as the parts of the city that look onto these canals (left) are called, have a double life. By day, they are quiet and industrious, their former factories now converted into lofts for artists and designers. But at night, they let their hair down. Dozens of bars, restaurants and pubs stay open from late afternoon until the early hours. The signs over the doors change with passing fashions, but the love of the Milanese for the Navigli is always the same.

The "Milan to sip"

The "Milan to sip" of a well-known 1980s television commercial no longer exists. What does remain, and indeed thrives, is the pleasure the Milanese take in getting together over a drink. They do it in their own style, of course. Milanese socializers drink on the hoof, in the latest bar with the newest cocktails and aperitifs. The bar has to be in the most fashionable district just off the city center, or on the way home from the office. For anyone under 40, the early evening happy hour is a mandatory appointment. The long Milanese nights are organized at these gatherings, as people wander - briskly, of course - from one bar to the next. And some people still insist that Milan is boring.

MANTUA

Palazzo Ducale, the dome
of Sant'Andrea and the bell tower
of the church of Santa Barbara,
on the other side of the Mincio,
welcome those who arrive
in Mantua from the east (left).
The city center of Gonzaga-era
Mantua is, with Venice, the best
conserved in Italy. The reputation
of the Po valley's capital of beauty
is reinforced by the story
of Isabella d'Este, an authentic
grande dame of the Renaissance,
and precursor of the contemporary
queens of the social circuit.
A woman of immense charm,
Isabella cast her spell over
Ariosto, Torquato Tasso, Perugino,
Mantegna, and even Leonardo
da Vinci. However, the great artist
never managed to paint her
portrait. What was her secret?
"She beguiled men without
affronting women, let herself
be adored while granting nothing,
and deceived everyone without
being unfaithful to anyone."
See for yourself when you visit
the superb Appartamento Nuovo
in Palazzo Ducale.

Piazza Sordello
For centuries, Piazza Sordello
with its cathedral dedicated
to Saint Peter and the Palazzo
Vescovile (above), was Mantua's
political and social hub. It has
never entirely relinquished this
role, for even today it is here that
Mantuans meet on the occasions
that matter. Perhaps they are
evoking the memory of the
enchanting Isabella,
or commemorating the infidelity
of Federico Gonzaga, who built
for his lovers, far from the city
center, the superb Palazzo Te
that today is the venue for major
exhibitions. The magnificent
16th-century construction
by Giulio Romano shows that
the adulterer was unconcerned
whether anyone noticed
his dallyings.

BELLAGIO

"Come and have a coffee with us," bawled the posters for a musical that enjoyed considerable success some time ago. And if the steaming cup is served in the coffee house at Villa Melzi (left), who is going to refuse? Looking out from the point of the peninsula that splits Lake Como into two, for two centuries Bellagio has been a resort that has welcomed the leading families of Lombardy, who have adorned it with splendid villas and parks. From Bellagio, you can take a boat to the other famous resorts around the lake to see at first hand the aristocratic homes, ancient fishing villages, long-established parks, and monuments hidden away in coves or perched on rocky peaks. The main thing is to come back at the right time. Coffee time.

TURIN

It's all in one photograph.
The Royal Palace (above: Palazzo Reale) reminds us of the prominent role played by Turin in the history of Italy, while at the same embodying the city's sober, understated style. The homeland of the Savoys yesterday, and of the country's leading manufacturing family today, Turin dislikes being the focus of attention. This persistent desire for privacy has helped to cloak the city in an air of mystery, and even magic. Piazza Castello is the location of a number of important buildings, such as Palazzo Madama, the Royal Armory (Armeria Reale), and the Royal Theatre (Teatro Regio). The austere porticos that line the square shelter some of Turin's historic coffeehouses. It is said that in the early 19th century, the Savoy monarchs used to find out what was being discussed around the tables of Piazza Castello to gauge the humors of the populace.

The Mole Antonelliana
The 167.5 meter-high Mole Antonelliana (right) is as emblematic of Turin today as it was yesterday. When it was completed in 1897, it was the tallest brick building in the world. Since 2000, it has housed the National Film Museum, a breath-taking journey from the days of magic lanterns to the special effects of the future. In its first three years, the museum attracted one million visitors. The Mole is the best balcony from which to view the city, and bridge the distance that separates Turin from the Alpine valleys where the 2006 Winter Olympics were held. The games will be another opportunity to revitalize Turin and its province.

Vineyards

Red is the keynote of the
photograph above, which shows
vines in the hill country around
Cuneo. It is emblematic
of Piemonte's destiny. The region's
celebrated winemaking tradition
offers a galaxy of great red wines,
from Barolo to Barbera, produced
on estates that are in tune to the
market's needs and developments.
What the market demands - and
gets - is quality, and respect
for natural winemaking methods.

Truffles

"The best ones are ours, the white
ones with a more delicate flavor".
The trifulau, as truffle hunters
are called in Piemonte, will brook
no arguments. They will defend
their supremacy against anyone
from the rest of Italy. What is
beyond doubt is the abundance
of these precious mushrooms,
which grow just under the surface
of the soil - the reason why
specially trained dogs are used
to find them - in certain parts

Chestnuts

Truffles are not the only specialty. Piemonte's busy autumn food and wine season always has a special place for chestnuts. Appreciated by rich and poor alike, they are served with meat dishes, or are used to create calorie-rich, but absolutely irresistible, sweets. The chestnut fair in the main square (right: a chestnut fair) is a long-established event in many towns and villages. Unsophisticated but compelling, the chestnut fair is increasingly an opportunity for serious tastings of the local wines. Visitors come from far and near for these events. Below: A cellar in the Langhe which, with Roero and Monferrato, is one of Piemonte's finest wine zones.

LAKE ORTA

Greece was the home of the Christian missionary named Julian, who in AD 390 chose the island in Lake Orta as the base for his evangelization efforts. It is strange that in Italy, a land of "saints and navigators," it should have been a foreigner - albeit a Saint who must also have navigated, given his origins - to discover this jewel of nature. But that's what happened. The mysticism of the past is still an integral part of life on Saint Julian's island. The nuns in the Benedictine convent are the island's most numerous community. Around the convent buildings are the old fishermen's houses, now converted into exclusive holiday homes that come to life only at weekends. The "Gateway to Heaven", as Saint Julian called it, is still open. But you don't need to go through it to get to Paradise. Just visit the island.

MATTERHORN

Once, the mountain chain that separated Valle d'Aosta from Switzerland had a uniform profile. Then Gargantua, the giant immortalized by Rabelais, arrived in the Breuil basin. Curious, he decided to see what was on the other side. However, the immense rocky bulwark crumbled under Gargantua's enormous weight. A single peak survived the disaster, and is now the Matterhorn, or Cervino in Italian (following pages). There are countless legends attached to the creation of "Europe's noblest crag." Although at 4,478 meters, it is only the third-highest mountain on the continent, it is undoubtedly the most famous, and much loved for its unique, instantly recognizable outline. Nowadays, the Matterhorn is friendlier, because several generations of mountaineers have climbed it. They have shown that the demons who were supposed to live on its slopes, and who would throw rocks at intruders into their privacy, do not actually exist. The route is clear.

Polenta and cheese
It's luxuriantly green, off the main tourist routes, and firmly attached to its past. Valpelline is one of the best-known cheesemaking zones in Valle d'Aosta (above right: the brand applied to genuine fontina, and a stall with a selection of typical cheeses). During the summer, mouth-watering open-air food fairs celebrate the marriage of cheese and polenta, the mountain folk's traditional staple, which is cooked out of doors in huge pots (right). These events are always very popular, and it is easy to see why.

Fontina

The cowherds and cheesemakers of Valle d'Aosta may never get rich, but as they tend their herds on high-altitude pastures, what they are producing is pure gold. It's the milk yielded by cows whose diet is made up entirely of herbs that have never seen agrochemicals. There are about 300 such pastures dotted around Valle d'Aosta each summer. Often, the milk is processed on the spot, to keep it as fresh as possible. The mountain dairies have all the equipment demanded by modern health regulations, but working techniques are the same as they have been for centuries. Thanks to this, fontina (left: maturing cheeses) has become emblematic of the entire region.

MONT BLANC

Armies from all over the continent threatened the borders of the Savoy kingdom and the rest of Italy. As a result, Valle d'Aosta became a land of castles, built high over the course of the Dora Baltea, the river that flows through the valley. Generally, castles were constructed within sight of each other, in a sort of relay of defense. As time passed, and the military reasons for castles became less pressing, many were converted into residences for the leading local families (above: the castle of Saint Pierre, near Aosta, which was radically restructured in the late 19th century). The valley's first and most impregnable bastion, however, was Mont Blanc, or Monte Bianco in Italian (right). Today, you can drive through the mountain in a long tunnel that runs from Courmayeur to Chamonix, or ride up it in a cable car, or make your way around it on foot or by bicycle. But try to imagine you are an ancient army. You're not going to get past Mont Blanc.

GENOA

Genoa is a town in a hurry,
yet it never seems to get tired.
Few other cities in the
Mediterranean have changed
their appearance over the last
15 years as radically as Genoa.
First, there was the work
for the Columbiad celebrations,
and the redevelopment
of the Old Port by architect Renzo
Piano (left: in the foreground
is the crane-shaped Bigo, which
features a futuristic panoramic
lift). Then came the makeover
for the G8 meeting. Finally,
a number of major projects
were completed as a fitting
commemoration of Genoa's
nomination as the European City
of Culture for 2004. Genoa
is a city of the sea, and such it
remains. It has prompted many
a sailor's grumble, and been the
setting for many an extraordinary
adventure. From Genoa, the eye
can see far and wide, well beyond
the physical horizon. And the mind
can dream without boundaries.

Palazzo San Giorgio
Just round the corner from
the Old Port is Piazza Caricamento,
where the 15th-century Palazzo
San Giorgio welcomes you to the
stately Genoa of great houses,
monuments, and art treasures
from the days when the city was
a great economic power.
The dazzling external appearance
of the building fails to impress
the Genoese. This was once
the home of the tax authorities
and the Banco di San Giorgio,
which administered tax revenues.
All in all, not that many locals
have affectionate memories
of the place. For non-Genoese
visiting the Liguria's principal city,
Palazzo San Giorgio has other
charms. Visitors, at least, can
admire it with a clear conscience.

CINQUE TERRE

Monterosso, Vernazza, Corniglia, Manarola, and Riomaggiore. Poets and travelers have sung the praises of these apparently banal places. But they are the nests of legendary birds, perched on sheer cliffs, or hidden away in bays sheltered from wind, storm, and - in the past - the incursions of corsairs.

The Cinque Terre national park gazes out to sea from the coast of Liguria's Riviera. Its villages, however, are inhabited not just by fisherfolk and sailors. Increasingly often, they are put at the disposal of vacationers in search of tranquillity in beautiful surroundings.

The seafarers of the past built their fortune on the seemingly inaccessible slopes behind their homes. Here, they cultivated the vine and its precious product, Sciacchettrà, a dried-grape meditation wine that Dante himself appreciated. Above: Rows of vines on the sheer slopes above Monterosso.

Via dell'Amore
Everyone knows that a heart in love can have explosive effects. It will come as no surprise that Via dell'Amore (right), a stunningly scenic path along the cliffs that separate Riomaggiore from Manarola, has explosive origins. For explosives had to be used frequently during work on the railway tunnels of the Genoa-La Spezia line in the early 20th century. The dynamite had to be stored well away from residential areas, and it was necessary to create a route from both villages to a secure area. When the trains began to puff their way through the bowels of the mountain, lovers from all over Europe took possession of the path.

PORTOFINO

Once a haven for ships in difficulty in high seas, Portofino was also a hideaway for more or less clandestine couples. They came for privacy, and to enjoy one of the loveliest views in the Mediterranean. It became the favorite haunt of those who demanded the very best. Then news spread, and the piazzetta where the fishermen hung their nets to dry became the world's Piazzetta. It turned into one of the most celebrity and autograph hunter-infested corners of the known world. Beauty attracts beauty. Nature has done her part so A-list stars like Demi Moore and Naomi Campbell are happy to do theirs in what seems like their second home. Unique, intriguing, exclusive, and mischievous, Portofino is a latter-day siren whose song enraptures the spirits of the most cynical Ulysses.

Wine

What did the sailors on the ships of the Genoese republic dream of returning home to? Not what you may be thinking. By contract, they were given shore leave to tend their vines. That could be the reason why Ligurian wines are so full of personality and unexpected nuances of flavor. The region has four distinct wine areas. In the east, is the Colli di Luni designated zone, which produces a full-flavored red wine. Then there is the Cinque Terre (above: terraced vineyards at Manarola), home of Sciacchetrà. To the west of Genoa itself is the Riviera Ligure di Ponente, with DOC Vermentino and Pigato wines. Finally, we have Rossese di Dolceacqua, almost on the border with France. One wonders whether those sailors spent more time dreaming of their vineyards, or the products of their cellars.

Fish and olives

Naturally, fish is a staple on Ligurian tables. It is also the main ingredient in a very well-known traditional recipe, cappon magro, a huge mixed salad of fish, vegetables, and eggs.
Right: The olive harvest at Taggia, on the western Riviera. Olives are another of the region's gastronomic treasures. Particularly in autumn, Ligurians hold glorious food fairs and feasts to honor olives and the extra virgin oil they yield.

Flowers and pesto

Sanremo is not just a popular holiday resort. It is also quite rightly considered to be one of Italy's main flower-producing towns (below). The climate and soil at Sanremo give the horticulturist a helping hand. The undisputed queen of the Ligurian table is pesto, a green sauce that is a perfect partner for pastas (left: a plate of trenette al pesto) and soups. The main ingredient is basil, which purists insist must be grown locally. Only then will its leaves absorb, and bring to your table, the true fragrance of the sea.

BOLOGNA

Known as "the learned city"
because it is the home of Europe's
most ancient university, Bologna
also boasts more then 40
museums and dozens of private
cultural associations and clubs,
often of great prestige. Bologna
(left: a bird's-eye view) has always
attracted scholars and artists,
so what is its secret? The city
does things seriously without
taking itself too seriously.

Two previous pages: Ferrara's
Castello Estense, the splendid
residence of the dukes of Este,
built in the 14th century.
The historic center of Ferrara,
which can be comfortably toured
on foot or by bicycle, has been
included on UNESCO's World
Heritage List for its profusion
of magnificent palazzos. Ferrara
hosts many important exhibitions,
often held in the halls of the
Palazzo dei Diamanti.

The Towers
There are 498 steps to climb
if you want to reach the top of the
97.5 meter-high Torre degli
Asinelli, but it is well worth the
effort. The panoramic view over
Emilia's regional capital is truly
breath taking. Standing next
to it is the tower firmly
established as its twin, the Torre
Garisenda. Originally, the Torre
Garisenda stood 60 meters high,
but it had to be lowered
in the 14th century because
of the instability of the terrain.
It took on its current squat profile
after this "decapitation," which
lopped a dozen meters off its
height. In the Middle Ages,
more than a hundred towers rose
into the skies over Bologna.
Some were built for military
purposes, whereas others were
erected in honor of families
that were influential, or aspired
to become so. Following pages:
Bologna's celebrated Piazza
Maggiore, the traditional meeting
place for the city's residents,
and often the venue for concerts.

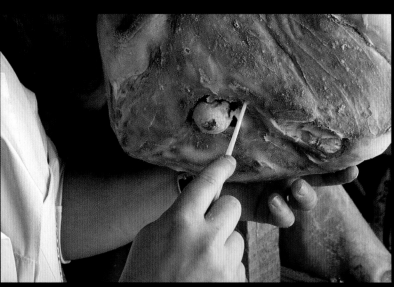

Ham and prosciutto

Parma ham, the town's famous prosciutto crudo, is a legend. Sadly, this unique and much-envied calling card has been ineptly copied all over the world. A celebrated product of Emilia's food and wine tradition (above: checking maturing hams, and a cellar), prosciutto crudo is only the best known of the fine cold meats that have made the region a point of reference for gourmets everywhere. Coppa, various kinds of salami, mortadella, and the delicious but hard-to-find culatello are made with slightly different techniques, depending on the production zone, but all are worthy to stand alongside Parma's celebrated prosciutto crudo.

Parmigiano Reggiano

Far from being just something to grate generously over pasta or rice, Parmigiano Reggiano (right: the cheesemaking process, and the characteristic rounds maturing) should be cut into large flakes, and enjoyed with an aperitif, starters, or just before dessert. Its nutritional qualities and substantial calorie content make Parmigiano Reggiano a favorite with athletes, who eat it before and during stamina-sapping competitions. Emilia's most famous cheese is a truly Olympic ring.

The important thing is that the pasta should be handmade by experts. You can call it tortellini, anolini, or any other name your imagination suggests, or local tradition might impose, depending on the province of Emilia you are in. Whatever the name, the pasta will be delicious. Emilia has a more passionate love affair with pasta than any other part of Italy. Whether it is long, like spaghetti and tagliatelle, short, or cut into shapes, and whether it is served dry, in broth, with a filling, like lasagne, or in rolls, like cannelloni, pasta is always the queen of the table. That is the only certainty. What filling or sauce awaits you at table, is a matter for the cook. Each has his or her own recipe, and each is the best.

FLORENCE

Think of a big city, like Milan, with its million and a half inhabitants. Then move that huge mass of people into a single building. Impossible? Not at all. That's how many visitors pass each year through the Uffizi to admire the most breath-taking collection of art works in the breath-taking city of Florence. There are actually two buildings that run parallel along the bank of the river Arno as far as Piazza della Signoria, dominated by the profile of Palazzo Vecchio (right). The name fails to do justice to such an important construction, dating from 1565 when Cosimo I de' Medici moved to Palazzo Pitti. In partial compensation, we might recall that the palazzo was originally called "dei Priori," then "della Signoria," and after that "Ducale". It was also the seat of the Italian parliament when Florence was the capital of Italy. Two preceding pages: A panoramic view of Florence crossed by the Arno. In the foreground is Ponte Vecchio.

Piazza della Signoria
The marble group of Hercules and Cacus, completed by Duccio Bandinelli in 1534, stands at the entrance to Palazzo Vecchio. It seems to be watching over Piazza della Signoria, the secular heart of Florence (above). This open-air museum offers art lovers a wealth of masterpieces of 16th-century sculpture, including Benvenuto Cellini's Perseus, Giambologna's Rape of the Sabines, and Ammannati's Fountain of Neptune, known to Florentines as Il Biancone (Big Whitey). There's even a fake. Right against the façade of Palazzo Vecchio is a perfect copy of Michelangelo's David. To admire the original, turn the page.

FLORENCE

Michelangelo's David
Moral strength and political
intelligence are what, for
Florentines, Michelangelo's David
(left) has represented over the
centuries. Completed in 1504,
and now displayed on a pedestal
at the Galleria dell'Accademia,
David spent his first 369 years
standing in Piazza della Signoria.
The contrast with Botticelli's
Primavera is only apparent.
The two best-known residents
of Tuscany's capital do share one
thing - absolute perfection.
A further three Davids are on
show in the medieval Palazzo
del Bargello: David-Apollo
is another expression of
Michelangelo's genius, and the
other two - the earlier in marble,
the second in bronze - are
by Donatello.

Botticelli's La Primavera
Beautiful? Extremely. Forever
young and only apparently naive,
she refuses to blush at being
the eternal focus of attention, and
guest of honor at a party where
many of the guests are world
famous. La Primavera (above),
painted by Botticelli in 1480,
is the best-known of the tens
of thousands of masterpieces
on display at the Galleria degli
Uffizi. Her exceptional co-stars,
in chronological order, are the
works of Cimabue, Giotto,
Simone Martini, Masaccio,
Fra Angelico, Paolo Uccello, Piero
della Francesca, and Verrocchio.
The journey through the history
of art continues with masters such
as Perugino, Leonardo da Vinci,
Mantegna, Michelangelo,
Raphael, Titian, and Parmigianino,
then on with Veronese, Tintoretto,
Rubens and the Dutch masters,
Caravaggio, Rembrandt and
18th-century artists like Guardi,
Canaletto, and Goya.
Each on its own makes the
journey to Florence worthwhile.
Are you sure you're not
embarrassed, Primavera?

Chianti

In Tuscany, the banquet
to celebrate the wedding of art,
city and superior wines never
quite reaches the dessert.
There is always some new,
unfailingly memorable dish
arriving at table.

Left: The 14th-century Rocca,
or fortress, of Montalcino, in the
province of Siena. It stands guard
over the vines that produce grapes
for Brunello, one of the region's
most illustrious red wines. Below.
The vineyards of Chianti Classico
appear to be laying siege to
Monteriggioni. It is no coincidence
that this town, perched on its
hilltop to the north of Siena,
is completely surrounded by
imposingly fortified 13th-century
walls. History tells us that they
were erected to defend
Monteriggioni from the attacks
of the Florentines. Still,
a "siege of the vines" is a much
more romantic proposition.

Cellars

There are 15 or so Wine Roads meandering through Tuscany. These are routes organized by consortia of fine wine producers to promote wine tourism in their areas. Vineyard and cellar visits can be combined with tastings of DOC wines, art visits and nature tours, as well as meals at Tuscany's excellent restaurants. The network of itineraries criss-crosses the entire region from north to south, and from east to west (above: a cellar near Lucca; right: Vin Santo, a dried-grape wine traditionally served with almond-based cantuccini biscuits). The network shows just how widely the vine is cultivated in Tuscany.

Lard

Sprinkle it with herbs, and leave it to mature in marble vats. That's how you make Colonnata lard (above right). What is now one of the driving forces of the Tuscan kitchen was once the staple food of quarrymen hewing marble just north of Carrara. Lard, nutritious and cheap, was placed in stone to protect it from wind, sun, and rain. This unusual, and indeed obligatory, method of conservation enhances the lard's flavors, creating a unique product. Who knows? Perhaps Michelangelo, no stranger to these quarries where he selected his blocks of marble, may have sampled the workers' lard.

PISA

If it hadn't been for the treacherous terrain it stands on, this would have been just one more splendid bell tower lending character to Tuscany's skyline. However, the less than prudent choice of location, which detached it from the Duomo, and set it on marshy ground, made the Tower of Pisa the one that "leans and leans and leans and never falls down," as a popular refrain of the past puts it. It has not fallen, thanks to recent drainage and consolidation work. Yet it might have stayed up forever anyway. Its relatively low 54 meters might have continued to grace Piazza dei Miracoli, the group of monuments that includes the Duomo, the circular-plan Baptistery, and the Cemetery, built in several stages from the 11th to the 14th centuries. The tower might simply have continued to cock a snook at scientists and engineers.

SAN GIMIGNANO

There are only 15 out of the original 72 left, but these are more than enough to give San Gimignano the skyline of a medieval Manhattan. The town's towers tell of its prosperous past, based on its strategic position. It stands on the ancient Via Francigena, which took pilgrims to Rome, exactly at the junction with the Via Pisana to the coast. Trade and wealth stimulated appetites and often bloody rivalries. Soon, however, these queens of the Tuscan skyline ceased to be built for defensive purposes, and assumed the more peaceful role of advertisements for the influence of their owners. There was one condition, laid down by statute in 1255. No tower could rise higher than the 54-meter Torre Rognosa that rises over Palazzo del Popolo. And none ever have.

SIENA

Like the claws of a crab, the shadows of the Torre del Mangia and the crenellations of Palazzo Pubblico reach out to pry open Italy's most famous "shell," Piazza del Campo in the heart of Siena (above). Surrounded by the city's most important civil and religious buildings, Piazza del Campo was laid out in the 14th century to be an amphitheater for games and tournaments of all kinds. It was by definition Siena's public space, and for centuries the only part of the city where the Sienese could indulge in gambling. Twice a year, on 2 July and 16 August, Piazza del Campo is the setting for the Palio (right), a horse race run by the city's contrade, or districts. The race is made memorable by the audience, traditional events, and open-air celebrations that precede it. Everyone is invited.

Olives
Little but good. When people talk about Tuscany's limited production of olives, in comparison with other parts of the Mediterranean, it is not to detract from its importance. Quite the reverse. The olive groves scattered over the hillsides and hinterland yield olives of very special quality, which are pressed to make an extra virgin oil of unrivaled excellence. Credit has to go to the soil, of course, but also to the firm, and in some respects mandatory, commitment to quality. Olive growing in Tuscany has very ancient roots, as do the oil-making techniques that are still employed today to guarantee the quality of the product. Tuscan oil is best consumed uncooked, the way it is traditionally served in most of the region's cuisine.

ROME

Piazza Navona

If you've been there, you'll have realized for yourself. Piazza Navona (above: a panoramic view) is more relaxed than any other public space in Rome. There's a party atmosphere, no matter what the hour of the day, or the day of the week. The generous space set aside for pedestrians, and the bars with their outside tables that stay crowded until late at night, are only part of the reason. Nor are the square's extraordinary monuments sufficient explanation (left: detail of the Fountain of the four Rivers, Bernini's Baroque masterpiece). What is it, then? Piazza Navona was conceived as a place of entertainment. It was here that the emperor Domitian constructed the stadium that bore his name in AD 86. It had a concave bottom that could be filled with water to stage naval battles. Since then, this part of the city has been the setting for an unending stream of fairs and celebrations of all kinds. Unforgettable ones, to judge by the smiles of the passers-by. Preceding pages: The Eternal City seen from the Pincio Terrace.

ROME

Roman window

Walk with your nose in the air. Just above the dazzling window displays, flower and plant-bedecked balconies make their own discreet contribution to Rome's reputation for being beautiful from any angle. But there's more. The curtains hide the rooms that are Rome's real seats of power. These are the reception rooms and offices, not far from institutions like the parliament building, where crucial decisions are often made in an atmosphere of discretion and elegance. Try to imagine what is going on at this precise moment behind that window, or on the terrace there might be on the floor above. In Rome, any answer could be the right one. It could be love, dinner, a political meeting, or a conspiracy. The merry-go-round of power sees stars of cinema and sport mingle with industrialists and musicians, literati, cardinals, aristocrats, and diplomats. Often, all at once. It has always been like that. That's how the capital draws you in.

The Spanish Steps

Via Condotti, the designer shopping street, Via del Babuino, with its 17th and 18th-century palazzos, and elegant Via Frattina all converge on Piazza di Spagna (right), one of the city's most popular and atmospheric open-air drawing rooms. Sitting on the 18th-century travertine Spanish Steps that lead up to Trinità dei Monti, the church at the top, is as much a must-do for visitors to Rome as a tour of the city's classical monuments. Here, you can observe the various aspects of modern-day Rome, a city of admiring tourists and schoolkids skipping class. All enjoying the tranquillity of a truly unique setting.

ROME
Trevi

When the architect Nicola Salvi designed it in the early 18th century, he created a masterpiece. More than two centuries later, the film genius of Federico Fellini used it as the setting for one of the signature scenes in La Dolce Vita, renewing and extending its fame. Fellini wasn't committing an act of sacrilege for the fountain of Trevi was designed to be a spectacular monument. Set hard against the walls of the Palazzo dei Duchi di Poli, it was actually commissioned by a pope, Clement XII. The imposing figure of Neptune dominates the group from his seashell drawn by two horses, each led by a Triton. Some say that to perpetuate his power, from time to time Neptune tells the Tritons to collect the coins that vacationers throw into the fountain. Of course, he doesn't need to stoop to this. And no one has ever seen the Tritons at work.

ROME

Forums

Anywhere else in the world,
a visitor overwhelmed by Baroque
and Renaissance attractions
of such quality and quantity
might forget about the city's
archaeological remains.
Not in Rome, though. The most
imposing traces of ancient Rome
are right in the center of the city.
You can't miss them. The Forum
(left) can be reached from
the Capitol on foot. It is rightly
considered the core of Roman
civilization, and the hub
of political, juridical and social
life in ancient Rome - many
of the buildings date from the
3rd century BC. Enough books
to fill several libraries have been
devoted to this area. We shall
restrict ourselves to going along
the so-called Via Sacra, past
temples, basilicas, courts,
markets, columns, and arches.
It feels as if you are entering
a videogame. In fact, it's all real.

Colosseum

Someone once fell so hopelessly
in love with it that he tried to buy
it. The gullible shopper concerned
lost a lot of money, an exemplary
punishment for someone who
thought love could be bought.
Luckily, today the Colosseum
(above) is in the pockets of every
European citizen on the five cent
piece. Inaugurated in AD 80
by the emperor Titus, it could
accommodate 50,000 spectators,
who came to watch sporting
competitions and gladiatorial
combats. There was even
a removable cover in case of rain.
Futuristic engineering solutions
have enabled the Colosseum
to survive to the present day
in enviable condition.
Think of those engineers as the
Colosseum's 2000th birthday
approaches.

DANIEL

ROME

Saint Peter's

Bernini's colonnade (above) seems to be concealing Saint Peter's, clasping it in a protective embrace. In fact, the double wing of 284 Doric columns is intended to symbolize the arms of the Church, open to welcome believers from all over the world. Bernini's researches while he was designing the colonnade enabled him to resolve the poor perspective of the dome, façade, and square. His intervention has brought everything together in a harmonious, if gigantic, whole. The colonnade also represents a link that joins Saint Peter's, the city of Rome, and the entire Christian communion around the globe.

Michelangelo

At first, he refused, courteously but firmly. By then in his 70s, Michelangelo wanted no part in the restructuring of the façade of Saint Peter's. When Paul III's request turned into an order, the artist finally agreed. But Michelangelo made it a condition that he should work for nothing, attracting ironic comments from his rivals. He was responsible for, among other things, the dome that "opens to the sky" (right: Bernini's later canopy is in the foreground). Two following pages: Detail of the frescoes in the Sistine Chapel, also by Michelangelo.

POMPEII

The Villa of the Mysteries (left: detail of a fresco cycle) in the archeological area of Pompeii may well offer the most atmospheric key to the secrets of Campania, a region full of contradictions yet extraordinarily rich in charm. In fact, Campania seduces like no other part of Italy. Pompeii is an obvious example of the Campania's many-faceted character. It combines the astonishing remains of a flourishing Roman city, buried by the catastrophic eruption of Vesuvius in 79 BC and today the most-visited archeological site in Italy, with the modern town that attracts a constant stream of pilgrims to the shrine of Our Lady of the Rosary.

NAPLES

Let us set to one side the stereotype that depicts Naples as beautiful but lazy, rich but chaotic, noble but oblivious of its past, and more interested in music and fun than in promoting its heritage. Pizza-and-tarantella Neapolitans still exist, but they are at serious risk of extinction. Naples has embarked on a new course, restoring its monuments and re-opening them to the public. The city is promoting scientific research and design, creating traffic-free zones, and making its magnificent parks once again safe to stroll in. Naples is again a city of culture, and even a popular destination for tourists. Left: Castel Nuovo, or Maschio Angioino, one of Naples' defining monuments. Begun in 1279 by Charles I of Anjou, it was comprehensively restructured after 1443 by Alfonso V of Aragon.

View of Naples
The imposing outline of Castel dell'Ovo (above: in the background) will melt the iciest heart. It has been doing so for some time. The first to land on the islet of Megaride was the Roman patrician Lucullus, who built a villa there.
Over the centuries, new arrivals in Naples - Normans, Swabians, Angevins and Aragonese - felt a need to leave their mark on the island, giving it walls, fortifications and wealth. The Neapolitans have kept its name. According to legend, the name Castel dell'Ovo (Egg Castle) derives from the Latin poet Virgil, whom locals regard as a powerful magician. Virgil is said to have hidden somewhere in the castle a talisman, an egg in an ampulla, in turn locked in an iron cage. The city would be protected from invaders as long as the egg remained intact. In fact, quite a number of omelets have been served since, but the flavor of the egg is still a matter for conjecture. Naples has never lost her soul.

CASERTA

It all began with the debts
contracted by a prince who never
made it into the history books.
His name was Michele Gaetani
di Sermoneta. Under pressure
from his creditors, he sold the
principate of Caserta to Charles I
of Bourbon. The year was 1750
and, in his enthusiasm, the young
sovereign pondered moving his
court to the new property. It was
a unique opportunity to throw
down the glove to his hated
enemies, the French. His palace
(the photographs shows the park
and a detail of a fountain) would
be bigger, more lavish, and even
more beautiful than Versailles.
He rejected a number of more
sober plans, and it fell to
Vanvitelli to start the job.
Work would finally end almost
one hundred years, and four kings,
after the first stone was laid.
The palace is 35 meters high,
and built to a rectangular plan
with sides measuring 247
and 190 meters. It occupies
an area of 28,300 square meters.
Scholars calculate that the overall
expense for the construction
of the Reggia was ten million
ducats, more than 20 times
the amount spent to purchase
the entire principate from the
insolvent Michele Gaetani.

AMALFI COAST

If you are wondering why the Amalfi coast (the photograph shows a panoramic view from Positano, with the Faraglioni rock needles of Capri in the background) has for centuries been under siege by poets, artists, princes, queens, celebrities, and limelight-shunning literati from all over the world, then you are asking the wrong question. Every visitor had - and continues to have - dozens of good reasons. Let's try to list them. Vietri sul Mare, the ceramics capital; Maiori with its long beach; the village of Minori and the remains of its Roman villa; Atrani and the palazzos built by the aristocracy of the Republic of Amalfi; romantic Ravello, suspended between sea and sky; Amalfi, which dominated the Mediterranean in the 10th century, and still has many remains from the period; solitary, savage Furore, wedged in its narrow gorge; and elegant, irresistible Positano, its houses built one on top of the other on the sheers cliffs over the sea. Fragrances, colors, crafts, cooks, fashion, and music are all created here, or come to the Costiera for a final touch of refinement.

Pizza

Tomatoes, mozzarella, anchovies, oregano, and olive oil. These, and only these, are the ingredients of a Neapolitan pizza. Yet all over Campania, pizza has its own local flavor. Wherever in the world you eat one, it is immediately obvious whether the pizza chef was born in the shadow of Vesuvius. The art of stretching pizza dough cannot be learned from a book. It is inborn, like the instinct that enables the pizza chef to select the most flavorsome tomatoes, or mozzarella from cheesemakers who use only first-quality milk.

Mozzarella

In Italy, a bufala (buffalo) is something that is false or untrue. It's a very common idiom that probably owes its origins to the endless attempts to copy the wonderful Campanian buffalo milk mozzarella. Actually, this marvel of the region's culinary tradition is made from milk that is so fatty and acid-rich that it is practically undrinkable. The secret consists in placing the curd in boiling water, but not allowing the high temperature to penetrate to the heart of the curd. In this

Fish

Before you examine the menu that the waiter offers you, take a stroll along the waterfront. Only by observing the fishermen unloading and selling their catch will you be able to enjoy your meal to the full. You will then be certain that the octopus on your plate is the freshest. Above all, you will have procured, without expense, the best possible sauce for your meal: the sight of your dinner being landed. Just this once, forget the rules of the Mediterranean diet. Campania's pastry chefs have just the thing to round off your meal, in the shape of a delectable filled puff pastry sfogliatella, or a diet-bending babà (below right).

CAPRI

Where nature could not intervene,
the human hand has. But given
the results, you are inclined to say
that both have done their very
best on Capri. Nature created
the marvelous Blue Grotto, and
the equally celebrated Faraglioni
rock needles (left: seen from
Monte Solaro). She also gave the
island the green of its flourishing
and very varied vegetation,
and the blue of its crystal-clear
sea. Humankind at once fell
in love with all this. One of the
first to come here was the Roman
emperor Tiberius, who had the
splendid Villa Jovis built and
lived there from AD 27 to AD 37.
Others who have left a profound
mark of love on Capri include the
Krupps, the German steel dynasty,
who arrived in the late 19th
century. Once they had settled,
they carved into the living rock
the panoramic path which bears
their name, and which descends
to the sea in a series of dizzyingly
steep curves. During the day,
residents and vacationers scatter
to the island's bays and paths,
but in the evening everyone meets
in the Piazzetta, the square that
is a magnet for celebrities and
celebrity spotters. Capri knows
how to stage social rituals, today
as yesterday.

ISCHIA

Ischia's beauty does not
overwhelm. Instead, it distributes
and shares well-being. The largest
of the islands in the Gulf
of Naples offers magnificent
panoramic views (above:
the ancient fishing village
of Sant'Angelo) and breath-taking
natural scenery. Its secret was
discovered long ago in the healing
waters that gush from Monte
Epomeo, the volcano whose
outline defines the Ischian skyline.
Humanity's desire for eternal
youth has encouraged the
construction of thermal spas,
beauty farms, and exclusive
temples to wellness. It has not,
however, canceled out the natural
savoir vivre of the local people.
In fact, it has fueled it. It's a nice
trick, isn't it? Following pages:
Paestum in the province of
Salerno, an extraordinary city
founded by the Greeks in 600 BC.

CASTEL DEL MONTE

There are no battlements or embrasures from which to fire on the enemy. It has no moat or drawbridge. The castle built by Frederick II at Castel del Monte, in the province of Bari, in the latter half of the 13th century has none of the features of a typical medieval fortification. It was erected for the sovereign, who is said to have intended to spend his declining years here hunting. Sadly, Frederick II died before he could move in. Castel del Monte, with its constant references to magical elements or the cabala, is a piece of architectural perfection. The repetition of the number eight, in the octagonal plan of the walls and courtyard, the eight towers, and the eight rooms on each floor, symbolizes the equilibrium of the universe, making Castel del Monte both astonishingly elegant and an endless source of material for legend. All contribute to its fame, which is well deserved.

LECCE

The capital of Baroque, or the Florence of the south. Whatever you want to call it, Lecce always has yet another secret to reveal in its architectural inventions, or its artistic interpretations of a theme. The procession of statues, friezes, pillars, capitals, and garlands that decorate the façades of Lecce's palazzos looks specially designed to deceive the eye, and distract attention from some controversial issue. For example, at the basilica of Santa Croce (above), popes, saints, and sovereigns stand next to bare-breasted women, and other emblems of prosperity. Similar distractions are on view at the church of San Marco (left), which features a lunette with the lion that was the symbol of the Venetian merchants who used it as a base.

ALBEROBELLO

The trulli of Alberobello (following pages) provide Puglia's most original, best-known postcard picture. These perfect, upside-down cones of stone provide coverings for the white farmhouses, and are unique in Italy. They bring to mind country scenes, and communities at work in the fields, bound together by firm ties of collaboration and co-operation. Today, many beautifully restored trulli have been converted into farm holiday centers, or are rented as holiday homes to visitors from the north. The ones who are not satisfied with an ordinary cottage.

TREMITI

Pay no attention to scientists who
tell you that the Tremiti islands
were once part of the Gargano
peninsula, from which they
were separated by a terrible
earthquake. The three islands
(above: part of the coastline
of San Domino) are actually
the exposed parts of three stones
that Homer's hero, Diomedes,
used to mark off the boundary
of his new kingdom, Daunia.
When he had finished the job,
Diomedes threw the remaining
stones into the sea, creating
San Domino, San Nicola,
and Capraia. Would you like proof?
The cliffs of the archipelago are
populated by colonies of albatross
(Diomedeae), Diomedes' sailors
transformed into birds to keep
eternal watch over his tomb.

Island of San Nicola
The island of San Nicola
is the entrance to the archipelago.
Its harbor is the only one that can
accommodate the tourists' boats.
Although it is the smallest
of the three islands, San Nicola
is the richest in history (right:
the 8th-century castle) and
monuments. Its ramparts,
cloisters, and abbeys tell
of a dynamic past that was also
pervaded by spirituality.
The aura of peace and well-being
still present is immediately
obvious to first-time visitors.
Just beyond the walls that
enclose the historic center
of San Nicola is the stunningly
beautiful abbey of Santa Maria,
erected by Benedictines from
Montecassino in 1045.

MATERA

Harsh. Off-putting. Inhospitable. Matera looks as if it was built to be abandoned by humanity. Yet Basilica's second city has become one of Italy's best-loved locations among writers, film directors, art historians, and even young couples in search of somewhere romantic.

The allure of a city carved out of the rock - friable tufa, but still rock - is stronger than the harshness of the environment. The grottoes have been inhabited almost without interruption since the Stone Age, and an entire community has even constructed churches underground (above: Santa Maria delle Malve, 9th century AD) as well as defensive mazes. Only a few decades ago, the Sassi at Matera were looked upon as a "national disgrace." Then came rediscovery, inclusion on the UNESCO World Heritage List, and the unreserved affection of contemporary thinkers and intellectuals. The city was reborn, from its foundations up.

ETNA

Calm and seductive when it is well behaved, Etna every so often likes to remind the world of its strength. It fires heavenward awesome chunks of fiery lava that then fall down its slopes in devastatingly incandescent torrents. At 3,323 meters, Etna is the highest active volcano in Europe. Its eruptions delight tourists, entice photographers, and excite scientists.

But the people who live here would happily do without Etna. Following pages: The snow-clad giant seen from Catania.

TAORMINA

Head-turningly beautiful, yet
never fully conscious of her role
as Sicily's seaside capital.
Perhaps unwittingly, Taormina
has saved herself. She has
resisted the siren song of those
who called for millions of cubic
meters of cement in the name
of prosperity. Taormina has
preferred to welcome
the exclusive tourists who
for centuries have been coming
here, to the east coast of Sicily,
by converting her most beautiful
palazzos (above: the garden
of the Hotel San Domenico,
a former 15th-century monastery),
her noble homes, and even her
farm estates. There has been
no large-scale recourse
to cosmetic surgery. "We're just
a hillside village with a sea view,"
her inhabitants seem to be saying
with a certain feigned modesty.
But what a view, and what
a village.

The Greek Theatre
Don't be deceived by appearances.
Despite the obvious intervention
of Roman architects in the
1st century AD, Taormina's Greek
theatre (right) has much older
origins. Besides, 300 years before
Christ, there were not too many
residents of the Eternal City
to be seen in these parts.
Carved into the hillside over
the city, with a panoramic view
of Calabria and Etna's looming
cone, the theatre is still admired
for the perfection of its acoustics.
Nothing could be more natural
than to watch outstanding
theatrical and musical
performances from a seat on
these tiers. That is precisely
what happens every summer,
and the program always features
works by the great classical
Greek playwrights.

Following pages: The temple
at Segesta, 30 kilometers east
of Trapani, another marvelous
monument to the Greek presence
in Sicily.

PALERMO

Palatine Chapel

Let us make it quite clear
that as well as being powerful,
the Normans were also extremely
cunning. In their golden age,
they conquered kingdoms with
disarming ease. Unlike many
other conquerors, however,
the Normans did not destroy
the works of their predecessors.
Quite the reverse, for they
enhanced the most significant
features, leaving sufficient leeway
for the self-expression of scholars
and artists from all schools.
In this way, they obtained two
results. First, they earned
the gratitude of the peoples they
conquered, but did not humiliate,
and second they were able
to foster works of art that are
unrivaled anywhere. One such
is the Palatine Chapel (left)
at the Royal Palace, or Palazzo
dei Normanni, in Palermo.
Dating from the 12th century,
it has the plan of a western
basilica, Byzantine mosaics,
and the wooden ceiling typical
of an Arab mosque. The styles are
diverse, but they fuse with such
harmony that Guy de Maupassant
was moved to exclaim, "It is the
most surprising religious jewel
dreamt by the human mind."

Praetorian Fountain

Proud, as their very beauty
demands. Reticent, their gaze
is ever directed elsewhere, never
at their interlocutor. But they are
also extremely shameless.
Most of them flaunt their
nakedness to passers-by.
It is not hard to imagine why
the Renaissance Praetorian
Fountain (above) is also known
as the "fountain of private parts."
Much loved by local residents,
the fountain was intended
to adorn the garden
of a Florentine aristocrat, who
died before it was completed.
His heirs, out of prudery
or poverty, sold it to the senate
in Palermo for 30,000 scudos.
This was a vast sum for
the year 1573, but at least
in this case, some public money
was well spent.

RAGUSA

Sicilians are magical. First, they trumpet a well-merited fame as the custodians of one of Italy's most interesting collections of Baroque. Then they enhance one of their masterpieces by building a 43 meter-high neoclassical dome on top of an 18th-century building. Purists might turn up their noses at Ragusa's church of San Giorgio (above). Well, they can console themselves with nearby Noto, Comiso, and Palazzolo Acredie, whose splendors are intact. But this spectacular contamination tells of a city that lay off the beaten track of commerce over past centuries, yet still managed to renew itself time and again. On each occasion, it has risen again, lovelier and richer, even after devastating earthquakes. Ragusa has never lacked a sense of humor. That much is clear from the sniggering masks carved on the palazzos in the square in front of San Giorgio. The patron who commissioned them may have known that one day, someone would put a dome on top of the church.

PIAZZA ARMERINA

"Cover yourself, girl. You'll have people talking. I've never seen such a scantily clad girl on the beach!" How blissfully ignorant our grandmothers were! Even in Roman times, women played beach volley in very succinct bikinis, as we see from the mosaics at Villa del Casale in Piazza Armerina, which date from the 3rd or 4th century AD. Their unequivocal evidence is before our eyes in our photographs (right). Art historians hasten to explain that this is really underwear - the top is a fascia pectoralis and the lower part is a subligaculum - which was sometimes worn for taking exercise. It doesn't matter. No one can stop you imagining. Villa del Casale, however, has many other wonders to offer. How could you ignore the majestic Corridor of the Great Hunt, with its 60 meter-long mosaic?

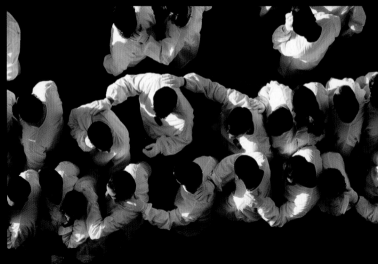

The feast of San Sebastiano
Every saint has a feast.
Sicily's great folklore events are
essentially religious in character.
Gaudy, lavish, and almost without
exception ancient, they are
extremely popular. Any tour
of the true Sicily should take into
account this intimately felt,
extravagantly expressed reality.
Above right: The feast of San
Sebastiano at Palazzolo Acreide.
The soldier-martyr Sebastian
was the pupil of the emperor
Diocletian. Betrayed by
an informer, he refused
to renounce the Christian religion
and was condemned to death
by bowshot. Since ancient times,
arrows have symbolized the
plague, a much-feared blight
in Sicily. But Sebastian was
a saint, and no evil could fracture
his faith, not even the plague.
That is the origin of his
veneration, which has never
flagged.

The feast of Sant'Agata
Is Etna threatening town
and country? Sant'Agata,
the patron saint of Catania,
will ward off the worst.
The remains of the santuzza,
martyred in the 3rd century AD,
were brought to Catania one
night in August 1126. The locals,
already devotees of the saint,
ran into the street to celebrate
her long-awaited return without
even bothering to dress.
That was the origin of the nudi
(right), the townspeople who each
year don white sackcloth,
representing a nightshirt,
and for three very intense days
accompany the huge silver image
of the saint round the city.

Tuna kill

There is no denying that the
mattanza, the tuna kill,
is a spectacle for strong stomachs.
In fact, it is not even a spectacle.
It is simply the undeniably cruel
climax of an ancient task,
historically vital for thousands
of families in western Sicily.
The tuna kill is an ancient method
of fishing. It involves using nets
to force the tuna to swim into
a pool, where the fishermen
are waiting for them. On fixed
days, tuna are killed in a festive
atmosphere that is not
immediately comprehensible
to visitors from other parts.
But for the fishermen, these days
drive off the nightmare of hunger
in the following months.
It is a feast of life, not a show
for tourists.

Salt pans

In Trapani, gold has another color.
White. It is extracted from the
sea, in the open air, and not dug
in the gloom of underground
galleries. However, this does not
mean that work in the ancient
salt pans (left), which have always
played an important role in the
city's economy, can be considered
easy. At least it is carried out
under the Sicilian sky, and not
in the possibly unsafe depths
of a mine. The white cones
of newly harvested salt offer
a spectacular sight at sunset,
when they are tinged
in a thousand shades of pink
glittering on every crystal.
At night, the pans are sheer
magic. Kissed by the moonlight,
they gleam like sheets of silver.
Quicksilver.

SARDINIA

Located in the middle of the
Tyrrhenian Sea, Sardinia has
a long history with no parallel
elsewhere. The most significant
remains are the Nuraghi (above:
the Su Nuraxi group at Barumini,
in the province of Cagliari).
These circular-plan constructions
bear witness to the pastoral
and agricultural culture that
established itself on the island
between 1800 and 1300 BC.
Left: The archeological site at
Nora, Sardinia's first modern
town, founded by the Phoenicians
in the 8th century BC on the site
of a Nuragic settlement.
Under the Carthaginians, Nora
became extremely wealthy,
and continued to prosper under
the Romans. It is quite possible
that Nora was the holiday
destination of choice of the
forebears of today's vacationers
on the Costa Smeralda. However,
the evidence is not conclusive.

Nuraghe
Sardinia's most celebrated calling
card is the sea (preceding pages:
the island of Maddalena, today
a national marine park).
This is quite appropriate, given
the transparency of the waters
around Italy's second-largest
island, the variety of its coastline,
and its wealth - some would say
surfeit - of excellent hotel
and accommodation facilities near
the loveliest beaches. Sardinia
is an island that is only too
capable of keeping up with
the times. It is a favorite with the
international jet set, who have
built sumptuous villas, crowd
the most exclusive hotels,
and clog the tiny harbors
of the marvelous Costa Smeralda
with their opulent yachts.
It is no coincidence that one
of the most popular pastimes
among ordinary mortals here
is celeb-watching. Some say
that the hobby was invented
in Sardinia.